WOLF STORIES

MYTHS AND TRUE-LIFE TALES FROM AROUND THE WORLD

SUSAN STRAUSS
STORYTELLER

GARY LUND
ILLUSTRATOR

BEYOND WORDS PUBLISHING, INC.

In honor of my friend Jean Half Moon, her generous heart

Published by
Beyond Words Publishing, Inc.
13950 NW Pumpkin Ridge Road
Hillsboro, OR 97124
Phone: (503) 647-5109
Fax: (503) 647-5114

Printed in the United States
Distributed to the book trade by Publishers Group West

Strauss, Susan.
    Wolf stories : myths and true life tales from around the world/
Susan Strauss ; Gary Lund, illustrator.
        p.   cm.
        ISBN 0-941831-84-1 (hard) : $11.95. — ISBN 0-941831-88-4 (soft) : $7.95
        1. Wolves—Folklore. 2. Tales. I. Lund, Gary. II. Title.
    GR730.W6S73 1993
    398.24'52974442—dc20   93-18382
                                                                       CIP
                                                                        AC

TABLE OF CONTENTS

INTRODUCTION

The wolf.
The mysterious one ... lingering at the forest's edge,
fire-lit eyes peering from the shadows.

This image of the wolf's shy, reclusive nature has caused some cultures to fear the wolf. Misinterpreting an animal that they did not understand, they often took the wolf's stance to be a preparation for attack. Since the Dark Ages in Europe, stories such as "Little Red Riding Hood," "The Boy Who Cried Wolf," and werewolf tales have portrayed the wolf as a shadowy, even demonic character ... an animal that needed to be caged or killed.

Fortunately, not all cultures have shared this view. In some ancient cultures, the wolf's reclusive nature inspired a sense of awe. They believed that this mysterious animal possessed knowledge that was beyond human reach and imagined the wolf to be a wisdomkeeper and spirit guide. These people took care to observe the wolf's habits closely. In their myths, the wolf is endowed with a special intelligence, alertness, strength, and perseverance. The wolf is shown to be a devoted parent and a responsive member in a cooperative pack society. Their myths present images of the wolf that are more true to the biological nature of the wolf than the blood-drinking demon in "Little Red Riding Hood."

To approach the mystery of the wolf, I give you stories, not answers . . . stories from wildlife biologists and mythologies from around the world.

MYTHS

In traditional Japanese folktales, the natural world is a source of great wisdom not found in human society. Prosperity often follows the character who is attentive to nature's teachings. At one time, the wolves of northern Japan were hunted to make room for horse farms, but today they are protected.

THE WOLF'S EYELASHES
JAPANESE FOLKTALE

There once lived a wealthy tradesman who had a daughter named Akiko. Akiko was generous and well-loved. Early in her life, her mother died and her father remarried a woman who was sharp-tongued and mean. Envy surged through every inch of the new wife's soul. She tried to weaken Akiko's grace and charm by ordering her to take on extra household tasks. Although the work

loomed before her like an immense mountain, Akiko worked until it was done . . . and she still managed to greet visitors at the door with a smile and beggars with a bowl of rice.

"Oh! She consoles every lost soul!" complained the wife to her husband at night. "If I didn't watch her, she would give everything away and make beggars of us all." The jealous, scheming wife pushed a wedge between Akiko and her father whenever she got a chance. "Maybe it wouldn't be so easy for her to give money away if it were hers. Every beggar knows where to get a handout, and they flock to this house. Are those the kind of people you want here when customers come to visit? You will see. Your customers will go elsewhere!"

No matter how hard Akiko worked, the wicked wife's complaints increased. When accused, Akiko stood silently before her father . . . head bowed . . . hiding the tears that welled up in her eyes. Being a proper Japanese girl, she never defended herself.

Still, the next day Akiko was back at work with a smile and good will in her voice. This only served to anger the wicked wife more. "I don't know why," she thought to herself, "but I hate her . . . her smile . . . her voice . . . everything." Then, on New Year's Eve day, her hatred finally found its way . . . "Oh, now look!" The wife flew into a fury. "Akiko cooked old rice for the festive meal! The God of Happiness will be offended. We will have bad luck for a whole year." The tradesman sent Akiko out of the house that day to make her own way.

Alone and forlorn, Akiko wandered from shop to shop. No one needed her. "Strange for a girl from such a family to wander the streets," they whispered behind her back.

Soon, she became weak from lack of food or a place to rest and begged at an innkeeper's door, "Please, honorable sir, I need some food. Will you take my quilted coat in exchange for some hot rice with fish and a cup of tea?"

11

"Give me your coat," said the innkeeper. "How can I know its worth if I don't sell it first?" He snatched her coat and shut the door before she could give him an answer. Trustingly, Akiko waited on the step.

Dressed only in her thin kimono, she waited. "That good coat should bring a few coins from the pawnshop," she thought, "and then, I will have a bowl of warm food." Once again, Akiko's spirits became bright. As she imagined the hot rice with fish, she went on to imagine working in a fine house with light-filled rooms and flowers for arranging. But her imagination grew thin as the waiting time passed on into the evening and the cold nipped at her through her kimono. She knocked at the innkeeper's door again. "Please sir, may I wait inside until your servant returns with the coins from the coat?"

"You again?" shouted the innkeeper. "What a nuisance you are. You will discourage customers. Get out or else I'll turn the dog loose on you."

But Akiko was already running . . . running from her shame, running from the glares of strangers in the street. It began to snow. Akiko grabbed an old sack from a garbage pile and kept running . . . running for the forest at the edge of town. "I would rather die in the forest than on any street in town," she thought. "Let the wolves eat me like people say they do. It is winter. The wolves must be hungry. In no time, they will find me and end my miserable life."

When Akiko entered the forest, she was somehow quieted . . . somehow comforted. She walked through the trees now hanging with snow. On and on she walked. With each step, she welcomed the imaginary wolf from the darkness that surrounded her.

Now, deep in the forest, she suddenly heard a slow growl. Crouched low and cautious . . . a wolf crept from the shadows. Akiko dropped to her knees, "Wolf, swallow me." The wolf circled back upon its tracks but never dropped its gaze. "I don't

eat human beings," it said. "Real human beings are rare . . . but you surely are one."

At once, Akiko became curious. "How can you tell that I'm really human?" she asked.

"Through my eyelashes I can see who you are," said the wolf. "Here, take these two. When you are walking in a town, look through them and you will see the truth. Do not trust whatever someone tells you. Trust only what you see through my lashes."

Akiko thanked the wolf and set off at once to the nearest town to see for herself how the wolf's gift worked. When she arrived in the town, Akiko seated herself at a busy intersection and watched people rush about their business with bundles and baskets. Some people were elegantly dressed. "These people look so respectable. Should I trust them? I'll try the wolf's eyelashes."

At once everything changed. Now the woman dressed in silk had a hen's head sticking out of her kimono, jerking greedily as if

pecking for seeds. She was followed by several servants with the heads of mice and fish. A merchant strutted by with a pig's head emerging from his fine kimono. Across the street, another merchant poked his fox's head from a doorway . . . his eyes darted quickly back and forth about the street. Not one human being walked among the crowd.

Akiko was ready to leave in despair when she saw a poor woodworker who did not change when she looked at him through the wolf's eyelashes. She followed him down the street and out into the country. When she caught up to him near his home, the woodworker said, "Who are you? You have been following me like a ghost!"

Akiko told him her story, and the woodworker took her into his home and fed her . . . although he had little to share. In time, Akiko grew strong. In time, they built a beautiful inn out of his small home. And in time, they fell in love.

Then one day, Akiko found a spring nearby, magically flowing with a fine rice wine. People came from miles around to visit the inn with this famous fine wine, and soon their business prospered.

Always, Akiko had a bowl of hot rice with fish for passing beggars and monks. One such beggar wept at her generosity. "Oh," he said, "years ago I turned out my own daughter, who was as generous as you. And now, who knows if she still lives. Oh, I deserve this hard luck, which is an equal match for my once hard heart." This beggar was, of course, Akiko's own father. Akiko forgave her father and told him the story of how the wolf's special way of seeing saved her. Akiko's father came to live with her and her new husband and to care for his new grandchild . . . often retelling the family story of the wolf's eyelashes.

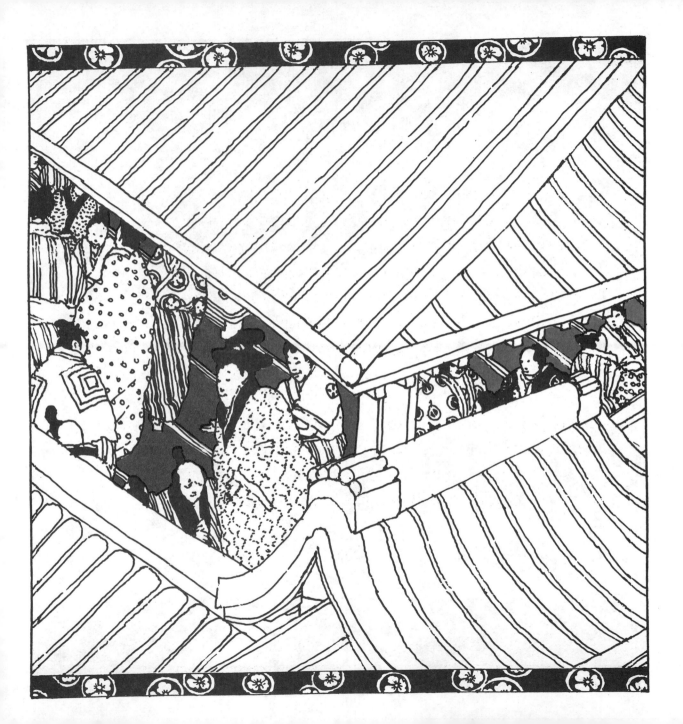

My friend Jean Half Moon is Nez Perce. She was raised by her grandmother, White Wolf, who was named after her spirit guide. Once Jean said to me, "When I was a child I was sent off to school. They read "Little Red Riding Hood" to us, and I thought . . . 'No, that's not right! That's not the way they are. Wolves are like us. They live in a tribe and know how to take care of each other.'"

SHE WHO LIVED WITH WOLVES
LAKOTA (SIOUX), NATIVE AMERICAN

She was Sioux, and she was mistreated by her husband. She spoke of it with others in her tribe, but she was not heard . . . and so, she . . . left her tribe in the dead of winter . . . in the dead

of winter . . . when all was frost and the wood was wet and all wild green things to eat were asleep underground. Still, she left her people in the dead of winter and wandered across the frozen land.

That night, she found shelter in a cave. A pack of wolves discovered her while she was sleeping and lay close around her to keep her warm. In the days to come, they hunted for her and taught her their way . . . the way of the wolf.

As the years passed, someone from her tribe found her and she was invited back . . . but she had changed. She was a shaman . . . a medicine woman . . . and she had no fear of death.

The medicine man of the tribe was jealous and didn't believe in her powers. He decided to challenge her. He threw the spirit power of buffalo at her in tufts of buffalo hair. She withstood it. He threw a horde of angry bees at her. She withstood it. Then, he threw maggots at her. She weakened for a moment. Then, she regained her strength and threw back grasshoppers . . . attacking like a hundred little blades . . . killing him instantly.

23

Throughout Western civilization, stories are told about she-wolves nurturing and raising heroes. Perhaps it is because wolves have so few offspring, reproducing only when there is enough food to support their young, that they are such devoted parents. The Persians, who were a nomadic society of warriors, may have seen the similarities between their community and that of the wolves.

SPAKO, THE WOLF GODDESS
PERSIAN FOLKTALE

In Persia, over two thousand years ago, a son was born to King Cambyses. Soon after the child was born, the queen, his mother, died. A call was sent out throughout the kingdom for a woman who could nurse the child and save his life.

Spako, the wolf goddess, heard the call and raced through the night until she came upon the castle walls. At once, she transformed herself into a woman. Fur fell from her form, and her body shook and stretched until a woman of great beauty stood where there had once been a wolf. Of her animal body, only her deep she-wolf eyes remained.

When she entered the court, King Cambyses was at once taken by her beauty. As the chosen queen, Spako was led to the chamber where the child slept. Alone with the king's child, she transformed herself back into a she-wolf and nursed the boy with wolf's milk. Cyrus, the young prince, grew to be a man of such strength, intelligence, and endurance that none of the surrounding kingdoms could resist his drive to form an empire. In his lifetime, Cyrus established the Persian Empire ... pushing the range of his once-small kingdom from India to Libya ... from the Persian Gulf to the Caspian Sea.

Two wolves, Gere and Freke, always guarded the throne
of Odin, the father god of Nordic tradition. The wolves earned
this position of honor because their strength and ferocious loyalty
were unmatched by any other animal. The wolf's place as the
predator in the chain of life was also respected by Norse culture.

Skoll and Hati, the Swallowers
Norse Myth

In the beginning, when the Asagods were bringing the first sense of order into the world . . . Sol and Mani, two beautiful children, were taken from their father and sent into the sky to drive the golden chariots of the sun and moon. The Asagods gave

the children this task in order to punish their father . . . for he bragged about their beauty constantly.

At first, Sol and Mani wandered where they willed throughout the sky. But their path was sent into a counting of the days and years by the hag of death, Gulveig. She unleashed two wolves into the world, Skoll and Hati. The two leapt into the sky to swallow the sun and the moon, but neither Skoll nor Hati could catch the sun or the moon. It is told by Saga, the goddess of story, that if they ever catch the sun and moon and swallow them, the world will come to an end.

But it is just because Skoll and Hati chase the sun and the moon that they move . . . and because they move, all of life on earth is moving.

Unlike Prokofiev's well-known tale, "Peter and the Wolf,"
traditional Russian fairy tales often cast the wolf as the hero.
It is the wolf who carries the characters across vast distances, shows
them the way out of the dark forest, and knows things that other
animals do not. Perhaps it is because the wolf survives the long,
cold Russian winters that it knows that what seems to be
an end is only the beginning.

THE FIREBIRD,
YOUNG IVAN, AND THE GRAY WOLF
RUSSIAN FAIRY TALE

Once an extraordinary tree grew in a king's garden. So magnificent was this tree that it produced apples made of gold. But one day, the king noticed that something was wrong.

Every morning, a few more apples had disappeared from the tree. His watchmen were unable to find the thief, and soon the king became ill and would take no food.

"Do not grieve, Father," said his three sons. "We will watch the tree throughout the night." The eldest son stayed up on the first night and the second son on the next. But as the night drew on, their eyes grew heavy, and each fell asleep. Still, they reported to their father the next morning, "The thief was not there; I am ready to swear. I did not close my eyes one wink."

Now, the third son, Ivan, offered to watch. "Ha!" his brothers cackled, their arms folded boldly across their chests. "What a waste of time that would be," they said, for Ivan was young.

But that night, young as he was, Ivan stayed awake. He put sticks between his eyelids. He threw water on his face. Then, deep in the dark of night, his hopes came ablaze. It was the thief. And not a thief at all, but a bird . . . a Firebird! . . . more colorful and light than all the king's castle halls lit with a thousand candles bright! Ivan jumped and plucked a feather before the bird flew away. The next morning, he presented it to his father. Each son vowed to recover the bird, and each set out in a different direction.

Young Ivan traveled on a hundred tired roads. Whether the way was long or not, no one knows for sure, but it was warm, and soon Ivan got off his horse to have a rest. Ivan bound the legs of the horse together so that it could not wander far while he slept.

When Ivan awoke, the horse was gone. "Oh, how can I continue without a horse?" he wondered. But he set out on foot. Whether the way was long or not, no one knows for sure, but when he became too weary to walk, Ivan sat down in the sweet grass to rest.

Softly . . . silently . . . a gray wolf crept out of the woods, head low, eyes alert. He spoke. "Why do you sit here so full of sorrow?"

Young Ivan told the wolf his whole tale.

"So! So!" said the wolf. "Sorry you are and sorry you might stay, but not for long, if you listen to what I say. I ate your horse,

but I couldn't have if you had let it go free. Still, you would never have found the Firebird with a horse. Only I know where it lives. Climb upon my back and hold tight."

They were off and running! Rivers and lakes and valleys passed by and deep evergreen forests in the wink of an eye . . . until at last they were standing along the wall of Tsar Afron's castle. "Listen!" said the wolf. "The Firebird is in the fourth room to the right. But when you have the Firebird in hand, take only the bird and leave its golden cage."

Ivan found his way and had the Firebird in hand. But just as he turned to leave . . . "Ah! A cage of gold. How can I resist?" The moment he put his hand on the cage, trumpets blew and guards appeared everywhere. "Hang you as a thief, I should," bellowed Tsar Afron, "but bring me the Horse with the Golden Mane . . . bring me that horse, and I will give you your Firebird."

Eyes downcast, Ivan returned to the wolf who said only, "Sorry you are and sorry you might stay, but not for long, if you listen to what I say."

Ivan climbed upon his back, and they were off and running! Rivers and lakes and valleys passed by and deep evergreen forests in the wink of an eye. At last they were standing along the wall of Tsar Kusman's castle. "Listen!" said the wolf. "The Horse with the Golden Mane is behind the last stable door. But when you have the horse in hand, take only it and leave its fine bridle behind."

But Ivan was young. He found the stable and the horse, but when he found the horse's bridle, fashioned with fine stones . . . "Oh! How can I resist?" The moment Ivan touched the bridle, trumpets blew throughout the castle and guards appeared everywhere. "Hang that thief!" yelled Tsar Kusman. "Yet, a thief I could use. If you can capture Yelena the Fair . . . ah! elegant Yelena . . . for me . . . the horse is yours."

Head low, Ivan returned to the wolf. "Ah!" said the wolf, "Sorry you are and sorry you might stay, but not for long, if you listen to what I say."

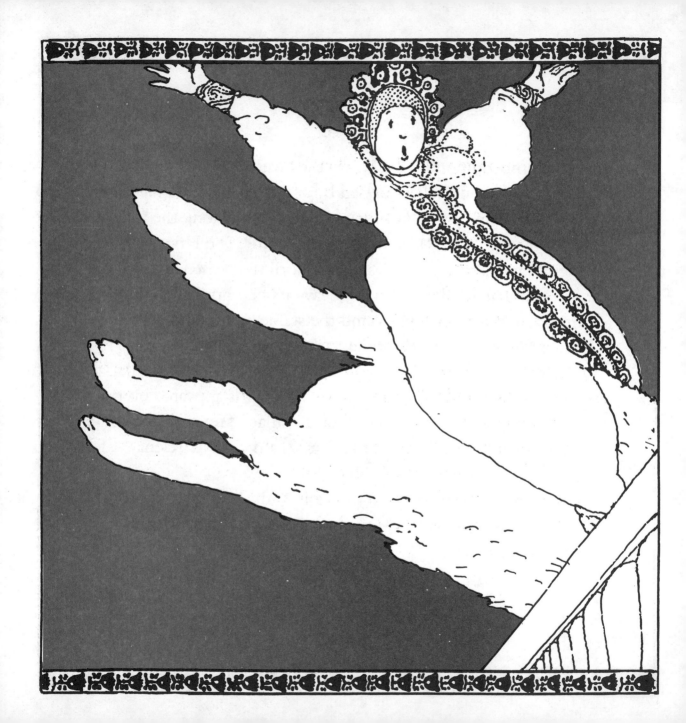

Again, onto the wolf's back. They were off and running! Rivers and lakes and valleys passed by and deep evergreen forests in the wink of an eye. At last they were standing along the wall of Tsar Dalmat's castle. "Listen!" said the wolf. "You stay here by this tree, and I will go inside."

In one leap, the wolf cleared the crown of the wall and crept into the garden. Watching until Yelena was alone . . . the wolf swept her up and onto his back and leapt the garden wall.

"Quick! Ivan!" called the wolf. "Climb on!" And they were off! Rivers and lakes and valleys passed by and deep evergreen forests in the wink of an eye.

Now they returned to each castle, and each time the wolf magically changed into the prize that each tsar sought. First he was Yelena and then the Horse with the Golden Mane. To each tsar, Ivan presented what appeared to be the prize. Then, late in the night, the wolf changed back into himself and met Ivan and Yelena along the road.

When the wolf found Ivan and Yelena, he saw how in love they had become. "I will leave now," he said, "but take care that you do not brag to your brothers about how you found the Firebird, the Horse, or Yelena." Ivan gratefully bowed three times before the wolf, and they parted ways.

As Yelena and Ivan traveled they stopped at a crossroads. Along the crossing road came Ivan's brothers. Empty-handed they were, although they had traveled far. "Hay! Ho!" called Ivan. "How good to see you." At once, Ivan began to tell of his great fortune. His brothers smiled all the while, but when the moment was right, they killed him and chopped him into a million pieces. They took the Firebird and the Horse with the Golden Mane and said to Yelena, "See that you forget all that you have seen."

The ravens were already circling above young Ivan's remains when the wolf found him. "Aoo!" said the wolf. "Sorry you are and sorry you might stay. If only you'd listen to what I have to say!" He snatched a raven from the air and said, "Fly and fetch me

the water of death and the water of life." At once, the raven flew. When she returned, the wolf ripped her child into pieces. He sprinkled the water of death on it, and its parts came together. He sprinkled the water of life on it, and up and away it flew with its mother. Now the wolf sprinkled the water of death on Ivan, and his parts came together. Then the water of life, and Ivan sat up . . . alive and well. "Oh, how soundly I slept," he yawned.

"Climb upon my back," said the wolf, and they were off! When they came upon the brothers, the wolf and Ivan tore them into bits and scattered them over the field.

Again, Ivan bowed to the wolf, and they parted. When Ivan returned home, his father was full of sorrow to hear how his sons were lost. But Ivan told him, "Sorry you are and sorry you might stay, but not for long, if you listen to what I say." When he finished telling his story, as I have just told you, the king was grateful and happy and lived long too.

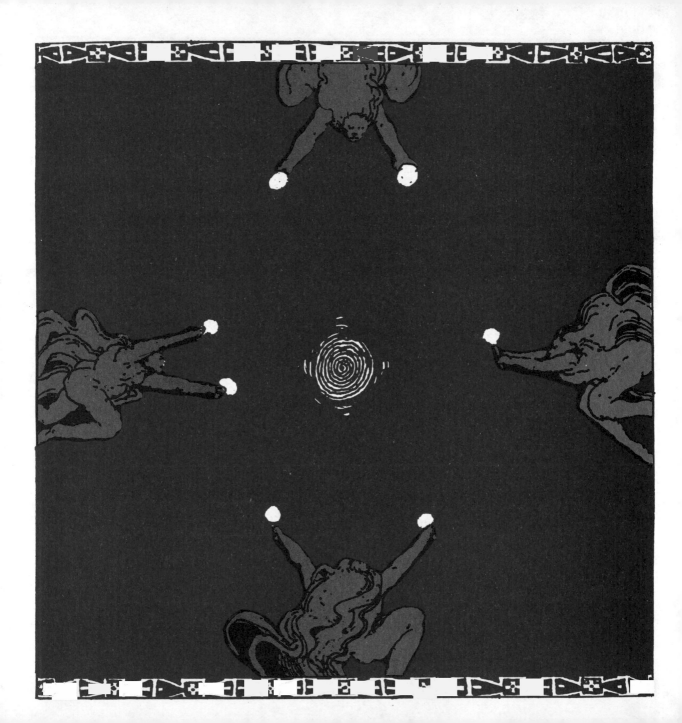

The Skidi Pawnee elders say that "each animal has something . . . some medicine to teach us." In their traditional ways, the wolf spirit is related to the change of the seasons . . . to death and renewal.

THE CREATION OF NORTH AMERICA AND THE WOLF

SKIDI PAWNEE, NATIVE AMERICAN

Before there was earth . . . before the dawn . . . before there was light . . . there was Tirawa, the great creating one . . . and Tirawa was calling across the heavens . . . calling the spirits along the sky path . . . calling the Powers of the Four Directions, calling them all together in one great creation council. Together they began to

sing . . . singing and shaking their rattles. And as they sang, winds began to whip across the heavens . . . winds whipped up clouds . . . clouds gathered in deep, dark pools. And then Tirawa took a rose quartz pebble and dropped it. Easily, it fell in among the clouds . . . and then the Lightning and Thunder struck right through the rose quartz. The storm began to subside. The clouds split and floated away . . . and below the creators of heaven was a vast ocean.

Now, the Powers of the Four Directions lifted their war clubs and hit these waters . . . spilling up great tidal waves . . . revealing the lands of the earth. But it was not until the Lightning and the Thunder Beings struck the earth that there was life in it.

Tirawa knew that the waters of the earth were not good to drink, and so again he began to call across the heavens . . . calling together the spirits . . . and the spirits began to sing . . . singing and shaking their rattles . . . and as they sang, winds whipped across the ground, carving deep ravines in the solid earth . . . and storm clouds began to gather . . . and poured their rains into these ravines. But it was not

until the Lightning and Thunder Beings struck into the water . . . and the water carried the sound of Thunder within its rolling that Tirawa knew these waters were sweet to drink.

And so on and on the spirits of the sky path sang our world into existence . . . all of them were there except for one . . . the forgotten one . . . the wolf.

Far off in the southeastern sky, the wolf star watched and wondered. Curious about the creation below, the wolf star sent itself down to the earth in the form of a gray wolf . . . and began tracking upon the land.

Now, the creation council decided to send someone down to examine their creation. They sent down Thunderer.

Thunderer was a magnificent being. He was made from the storm clouds out of the West. His mother, the evening star, wove for him a whirlwind sack. His father, the morning star, gathered stars from across the sky path and poured them into the sack. These stars would be the first human beings. Thunderer slung the

whirlwind sack across his back and set out across the earth. Each time Thunderer stepped down to the earth, lightning bolts struck the ground. Out of his blackened footsteps, buffalo leapt up and ran out across the plains.

At times, Thunderer would stand on the earth as a great giant of a man and set his whirlwind sack down. At once, human people would spill out. Some set up their lodges, and others ran off to hunt buffalo. Then they would prepare a great feast for Thunderer. Thunderer was delighted with these little human people. When the feast was finished, he set his whirlwind sack on the ground and sucked them back up inside.

In this way, Thunderer traveled on. All the while, the wolf was tracking his footsteps. When the wolf finally came upon Thunderer, he was sleeping up against the front range of the Rocky Mountains . . . using the whirlwind sack as a pillow.

The wolf crept up slowly . . . thinking that there was something to eat in the sack, he crept closer and nipped at the sack . . . he nipped it . . . pulled it . . . pulled it . . . pulled it loose from under Thunderer's sleeping head . . . grasped it in his jaws, leapt back, and ran off across the grasslands.

The wolf ran far into the south grasslands before he dropped the sack. When he was far enough away, he set the sack on the earth, and out piled the human people. They set up their lodges, and some went off to hunt buffalo.

One old woman noticed the wolf. Thinking he was Thunderer in another form, she fed the wolf some dried buffalo meat. The wolf lapped it up. But the others, who had gone off to hunt buffalo, couldn't find any buffalo, and they began to wonder . . . "Who is that strange animal? An evil spirit?"

Then, from across the plains, they saw Thunderer coming . . . with his long lightning strides. At once they thought, "That animal . . . he must be an evil spirit!" They ran back to the old woman's lodge. They lifted their arrows and shot. The wolf whined . . . loped for a step or two . . . and dropped.

Then, outside the lodge, they heard a powerful storm gathering . . . *SSSSHHHOOO!* They piled out of the lodge, and there before them stood Thunderer.

Thunder said, "Ooooh. Look what you have done. You have killed an animal you did not understand. Because you have killed something before you understood it, death, another mystery, will now live in its place. Ooooh, I would have carried you forever in my whirlwind sack, but now death will live with you in the world."

Thunderer told the people to take the skin of this animal and make a sacred bundle from it and hang it in their lodge, facing the North Star. He told them that soon there would be many animals like this one. They will be called Skidihk, the wolf. "And you," he said, "you will be called the Skidi Pawnee, the Wolf People. In your name, and in death . . . you will always remember to respect the mysterious one."

TRUE-LIFE TALES

A Wolf at the Door

When a wolf has figured out how to escape from a pen, it won't stay caged for long.

Once, such an escape artist was among a group of wolves being studied by the famous wolf biologist Dr. David Mech. During the course of their research, Dr. Mech and others often let the wolf out of its cage into a larger pen. The wolf watched as the cage door slid up and down on its cable wires. Up the door would go, and back the cable wire would pull along the eight-foot-high horizon ridge of the pen wall. At one point along the ridge, the wire cable arched, ever so slightly, to the inside of the pen.

The wolf jumped for it and grabbed the cable with its teeth. The door slid up . . . and then down . . . once the wolf let go of the wire. But the wolf was not discouraged. It repeated the same eight-foot jump and cable-grab again and again until the door stuck . . . and the wolf was gone.

"Wolves don't learn tricks as easily as dogs do," says Dr. Mech. "But that's not because they can't. They're just not interested in tricks, but they will watch some event going on in their world and take from it their own ideas to solve a new problem in a different situation. Wolves are more clever than dogs when it comes to problem-solving."

WOLF PARENTS

Early trappers in the Northwest Territory would steal wolf pups from their dens at an early age to raise them as pack dogs. There are accounts of wolf parents trying to sneak into a trappers' camp and rescue their pups. Even when they were shot at, they kept coming back.

ONE OF THE PACK

A wildlife biologist was studying a group of wolves that had been raised together in captivity from birth. They regarded each other as members of a pack, and by the usual signs of ears, tails, and posture, they seemed to accept the biologist, who visited their enclosure regularly, as part of their pack.

One day, the biologist wanted to see if a choke-chain leash could be used when moving wolves from one pen to another. He entered their enclosure and put a choke chain around the neck of one of the females.

All of a sudden, she panicked. She began to twist and shake her head . . . trying to get free of the chain. Then she ran full speed to the other side of the enclosure . . . trying to break the chain. When she hit the chain's end, she flopped over on her back. Then she got up and ran full speed again to the other side of the enclosure. Again the chain cinched tight around her neck and her legs slid out from under her.

"She is going to strangle herself if I don't do something,"

thought the biologist. So, pulling himself along the chain, he made his way up to the she-wolf, grabbed her by all four legs, flipped her over, put his knee on her chest, and began to loosen the leash . . . when he noticed . . . all of the other wolves had surrounded him. *GRRRR* . . . a threatening growl rattled across their bared white teeth. "This is it. I'm down," thought the biologist. He knew that a wolf can break an elk's leg bone as easily as it could snap a twig.

Just at that moment, one of the wolves leapt onto his leg, surrounding his ankle with its open mouth of bared teeth, and growled. Then the wolf jumped back and whined. Suddenly he leapt back onto the biologist's leg with his bared teeth and growled again. Then he jumped back and whined again. He looked like a man who was so frightened he couldn't scream.

In that moment, the biologist pulled off the leash and released the she-wolf. At once, the wolves were up wagging their tails and making sure she was OK. They went about their business as if the whole incident had never happened. The biologist stood quietly and watched them. Treated as a member of their family, he had been corrected without being harmed.

BABYSITTING? OH, BROTHER!

Up to Ellesmere Island . . . six-hundred miles from the North Pole . . . wolf biologists Dave Mech, Janet Packard, and Bob Ream went to observe Arctic wolves—wolves that had never seen human beings before.

They set up their observation post on a ridge overlooking the den. They would sit and watch everything the wolves did . . . and the wolves would sit and watch everything the humans did. Now and then, and especially just before the hunt, the wolves would come over to get a closer sniff at the humans. Were they being friendly, curious, or concerned about whom they were leaving behind?

One month earlier one of the females had given birth to four pups, and she was now strong enough to hunt with the pack. Who watched over the pups while she was gone? Why, none other than the playful, jump-waggle-and-roll older brother that the biologists called Waggle 'n' Roll.

The pups loved him! They'd tear into the valley at a cool wolf gallop . . . wrestle and love-bite until big brother would roll over and give up . . . then, up again to start the game over.

The sun never sets during Arctic summer nights. Yet the air hangs with the sweet stillness of night, and the land seems very big and lonely. One such night, Waggle 'n' Roll and his cub pack fell asleep while the others were off hunting. Soon a few pups woke up . . . and then a few more. Waggle 'n' Roll slept on, so the pups decided to go exploring without him. They wandered up to visit the humans. Then they wandered up over the ridge and disappeared.

When Waggle 'n' Roll woke up and realized that his brothers and sisters were nowhere to be seen, he was frantic. His ears back, he began sniffing all around the valley. He howled. He sniffed all around the valley again. He howled . . . where could they be? He raced up to the den and sniffed. He howled again and moped around, dragging his body like a wet towel.

Then, all of a sudden, the pups came into view racing around up the ridge, and down into the valley they charged. They greeted their older brother wildly . . . jumps and love-bites and lots of waggle and roll. Babysitting? Oh, brother!

Resources

Other Books about Wolves:

L. David Mech, *The Wolf*
L. David Mech, *The Arctic Wolf*
Barry Lopez, *Of Wolves and Men*

Organizations for Education and Advocacy Regarding Wolves:

The Wolf Fund: Learn how you can help return the wolf to its native home. P.O. Box 471, Moose, WY 83012, (307) 733-0740

Defenders of Wildlife: (202) 659-9510

The Wilderness Society: Sets aside land for wolf reintroduction and does advocacy related to the Endangered Species Act. 900 17th St. NW, Washington, DC 20006-2596, (202) 833-2300

The International Wolf Center: Offers memberships, research, speakers' bureau, wolf weekends, wolf-center activities, exhibits. 1396 Highway 169, Ely, MN 55731, (218) 365-HOWL

The United States Fish and Wildlife Service: Contact your local office.

Adopt a Wolf: You can contribute to the housing, feeding, and care of the thirty-eight wolves living on the sixty-five-acre **Wolf Haven** in Tenino, Washington. For a $20 to $35 contribution you will receive a parchment certificate along with biographical information and a color photo of your adopted *Canis lupus.* 1-800-448-WOLF

Mission Wolf: P.O. Box 211, Silver Cliff, CO 81249, (719) 746-2919

OTHER BOOKS FROM BEYOND WORDS

COYOTE STORIES FOR CHILDREN

THE GREAT CHANGE

CEREMONY IN THE CIRCLE OF LIFE

NATIVE PEOPLE, NATIVE WAYS SERIES

AUDIO TAPES FROM SUSAN STRAUSS

COYOTE GETS A CADILLAC

TRACKS, TRACKS, TRACKS

WITCHES, QUEENS & GODDESSES

THE BIRD'S TALE

YIDDISH & HASSIDIC TALES

For a free catalogue of children's books and tapes, write to Beyond Words Publishing, Inc., 13950 NW Pumpkin Ridge Road, Hillsboro, OR 97124 or call (503) 647-5109